/Beau-ty (/ˈbyoodē/) - noun - Being the best possible version of yourself, inside & out.

BEAUTY IS AN INSIDE JOB: 30 PRACTICAL MAGIC LESSONS FROM THE BEWITCHING WORLD OF BURLESQUE

A GAL'S GUIDE TO FINDING YOUR INNER MAGIC BY BEING THE BEST VERSION OF YOURSELF INSIDE AND OUT

The world is full of magic things, patiently waiting for our senses to grow sharper.

—*W.B.Yeats*

Beauty begins the moment you decide to be yourself.

—*Coco Chanel*

Written by Kitty Kat DeMille & Julia Reed Nichols

© 2022 Do Right Industries
PRINT ISBN: 978-0-578-35052-3
EBOOK ISBN: 978-0-578-35053-0

FOREWORD	9
INTRO JULIA	10
INTRO KAT	12
Journal Prompt #1	15
AFFIRMATION	15
THE BASICS	16
1 - BEAUTY IS AN INSIDE JOB	18
Journal Prompt #2	25
AFFIRMATION	25
2 - HAPPY IS AS HAPPY DOES	27
Journal Prompt #3	29
AFFIRMATION	29
3 - YOU BEING YOU IS A GIFT	31
Journal Prompt #4	36
AFFIRMATION	36
4 - IT'S OKAY TO SPARKLE	38
Journal Prompt #5	42

AFFIRMATION	42
5 - KNOW YOUR WORTH, THEN ADD TAX	44
Journal Prompt #6	47
AFFIRMATION	47
6 - STOP APOLOGIZING FOR YOUR CHOICES	49
Journal Prompt #7	52
AFFIRMATION	52
BODY LOVE	**54**
7 - BE YOUR OWN GREATEST LOVER	55
Journal Prompt #8	57
AFFIRMATION	57
8 - WORDS HAVE MAGIC; THAT'S WHY IT'S CALLED SPELLING	59
Journal Prompt #9	64
AFFIRMATION	64
9 - STRIKE A POWER POSE…THERE'S NOTHING TO IT	66
Journal Prompt #10	71
AFFIRMATION	71

10 - SHAKE THAT ASS	73
Journal Prompt #11	78
AFFIRMATION	78
11 - PLAY DRESS UP WITH YOUR LIFE	80
Journal Prompt #12	85
AFFIRMATION	85
12 - MOTHER NATURE IS YOUR BESTIE	87
Journal Prompt #13	89
AFFIRMATION	89
13 - SMOKE & MIRRORS ARE YOUR FRIENDS	91
Journal Prompt #14	93
AFFIRMATION	93
14 - BE NAKED MORE	95
Journal Prompt #15	98
AFFIRMATION	98
15 - SILENCE IS SEXY	100
Journal Prompt #16	103

AFFIRMATION	103

LIFE IMPROVEMENT — **105**

16 - OWN THE ROOM BEFORE YOU ENTER IT	106
Journal Prompt #17	108
Affirmation	108
17 - BE A KICKASS BACK UP DANCER	110
Journal Prompt #18	112
AFFIRMATION	112
18 - DOING IT IN HEELS BACKWARD	114
Journal Prompt #19	117
AFFIRMATION	117
19 - IT'S OKAY TO MAKE OTHERS JEALOUS; YOU'RE ACTUALLY GIVING THEM A GIFT!	119
Journal Prompt #20	121
AFFIRMATION	121
20 - ROCK & ROLL CAN SAVE YOUR SOUL	123
Journal Prompt #21	126
AFFIRMATION	126

21 - IF YOU CAN APPRECIATE YOUR ASSETS, YOU'LL ALWAYS SHOW A PROFIT!	128
Journal Prompt #22	129
Affirmation	129
22 - DREAMS ARE FOREVER & IMAGINATION HAS NO AGE	131
Journal Prompt #23	133
AFFIRMATION	133
ROMANCE	**135**
23 - RELATIONSHIPS ARE THE ULTIMATE LESSON IN WHO WE ARE	136
Journal Prompt #24	138
AFFIRMATION	138
24 - CONFIDENCE IS GRAVITATIONAL	140
Journal Prompt #25	143
AFFIRMATION	143
25 - WORK THE TEASE	145
Journal Prompt #26	147
AFFIRMATION	147
26 - EMBRACE MYSTERY	149

Journal Prompt #27	150
AFFIRMATION	150
27 - SEX MAGIC IS REAL	152
Journal Prompt #28	158
AFFIRMATION	158
28 - PROTECT YOUR BOUNDARIES	160
Journal Prompt #29	164
AFFIRMATION	164
29 - IT TAKES TWO TO TANGO	166
Journal Prompt #30	168
AFFIRMATION	168
THE ONLY RULE	**170**
30 - CHANGE IS THE ONLY CONSTANT	171
Journal Prompt #31	173
AFFIRMATION	173
~ Follow Our Adventures ~	**176**

FOREWORD

Our souls are eternal. Female, male, & other gender role identities are something tried on & cast off like pieces of clothing.

This book was written by two souls who at this moment identify with being females. These are the lessons we've discovered through our Magical Striptease adventures inspired by the glittery Burlesque Stars who've helped us along the way. The stories are specific to us, but truths are universal.

So, whatever your gender, race, or sexual preference on this go around, we thank you for listening to our tales, & we hope it helps you remember how bewitching you are! Happy revealing!

INTRO JULIA

In many ways, Burlesque is a business to me. It is my job as the founder of Pin-ups on Tour, a nationally touring Burlesque show, to know not only what people want to see but also what will keep them coming back for more. The brighter I shine, the brighter the women I work with shine, & the more people are attracted to what we are building. Positive energy builds positive momentum.

Through Burlesque, I have discovered a very powerful part of myself that has allowed me to be more fulfilled not only as a performer but also as a woman & as a business person. It also has been a tool for tapping into my intuition & divine femininity—the part of myself that truly knows what I want. When you have the confidence of a self-sufficient goddess, the RIGHT kind of people are drawn to your side. Your partners become people who admire your ambition & want you to show off your beauty. Your friends become allies, people who see what you have to offer is special in this world.

I had to learn these lessons the hard way, & maybe I'm still learning them in many ways. I've been married, divorced, engaged, & have dated just about every type of person out there. Through my twenty years of romantic experience & my ten years of Burlesque, I have learned how to attract people & how to let them go when needed. The invention of online dating has made it even more imperative that we set our boundaries & goals, & all this starts with knowing your worth & claiming your space in this world as a beautiful person who deserves all your heart's desires. Only invite people who want to be a part of your Magical world.

As you go through this book, emotions are likely to be brought up. We all have long-term programming around sexuality & beauty—if you were raised in a religious household like me, there might be some pesky shame that needs to be shed before you can fully step into this power. This book is meant to inspire you with some of the lessons we have learned on the road as traveling Showgirls.

One thing that helps me as I approach new ideas is to journal. I encourage you to break up this book. Read a chapter a day, take a little time to reflect on what you read, & write down your thoughts. Of course, this is beneficial at any time of the day, but I like to start my day with a little reading & journaling. I find that my mind takes the day to mull it over, & often connections are made that reinforce the new mindset I am trying to establish.

You never actually have to get naked in front of a crowd to benefit from these theories (although you may find yourself wanting to by the end of this book)— our only goal is for you to discover & celebrate the beauty in you!

INTRO KAT

To me being a performer is one of the most Magical callings out there. Our job is to entertain people, to make them remember that there is beauty in the world, & to help make them forget their worries for a moment so they can become reenergized with a zest for life. To bring a smile to someone's face is to remind them that there is FUN, & good, & sparkle, & shine out there.

That wonder exists around every corner, & life can be as extraordinary as you allow it to be.

I didn't always believe beauty was an inside job.

That's the thing with self-belief: it's a high-wire tightrope we always walk. There will be days where you believe you're beautiful, & there are days where you think you're a chopped liver. And both are true because it's the belief that makes it so! But hey, life is a journey of self-discovery, & my grandmother absolutely loved a liver!

My experience with empowerment has definitely traveled the spectrum. I spent ten years of my life as a bulimic despising my body for what it was not. Luckily with lots of self-work & energy healings, I changed that narrative to one of self-love.

This inner work led me to audition for the Santa Monica-based Burlesque troupe The Dollface Dames on a whim (something my high school persona would have never dared to experience). And, as fate would have it, during that audition, I met a pipsqueak of a singer/dancer named Julia Reed Nichols, & the rest, as they say, was history!

With a Bestie by my side, I discovered a witchy world of six-inch stilettos, whalebone corsets, thigh-high stockings, & getting naked in front of perfect strangers. Here you could be anyone you wanted to be, as long as you believed in who that was! So, with some rhinestones, the perfect shade of lipstick (Kiss a Vet by Pin-Ups On Tour), & some killer self-confidence, I've performed

Burlesque in thirty states (with Workin' The Tease, Pin-Ups On Tour, & The Green Light District) & stripped at some of the most notable strip clubs of Las Vegas & New Orleans.

Burlesque has taught me many lessons over the past decade, but at the top of the list is this—to be truly beautiful, you need to believe you are beautiful. Nobody else is gonna spend the necessary man hours on this quest of self-discovery.

As a Burlesque performer turned producer, I have seen hundreds of different performers of every shape, size, & age work a room, & the one thing that kills more than anything else is self-love. The more that entertainer adores herself on stage, the more the audience clamors for more. Yes, these enchantments are enhanced by feathers, rhinestones, & glitter, but at the heart of these spells is self-adoration.

So why choose to be a mere mortal when you can be a marvelous Magical Witch full of twinkle & light? Come & join the Glitterati. I can guarantee it's a Hell of a lot more FUN!

***

Journal Prompt #1

Why did you pick up this book?

AFFIRMATION

It Feels Good to Look at Myself

(Say this in the mirror until the phrase makes you smile)

THE BASICS

Workin' The Tease's 1st Photoshoot. Photo by William Kidson

1 - BEAUTY IS AN INSIDE JOB

> Beauty is not in the face; beauty is a light in the heart.
>
> —*Kahlil Gibran*

We want to tell you that beauty is an inside job.

In our years of building a Burlesque empire, we have encountered many movers & shakers in the Burly world. These women, & men, of all shapes & sizes, are comfortable enough to take off their clothes for perfect strangers.

Question: What gives these sparkly people the gumption to do so?

Answer:

CONFIDENCE

CONFIDENCE

CONFIDENCE

(And no, the perfect body was nowhere near the top of the list!)

Yes, we know you've heard it before, & maybe there have been times you've believed it, but if you're reading this book, we can pretty much guarantee that you're not believing it one hundred percent of the time.

So we're here to remind you that beauty is an inside job.

Let's embrace the world of T & A: Talent & Attitude. Sexiness is all about your personality, about being genuine & wielding that power you have of being you like an energetic Samurai sword. To the point of being Fucking Magical.

Confidence is sexy as Fuck & casts a spell on everyone you meet! Wear it daily in everything you do.

There are two types of people in life. On one side are the Drabsters. These are the people who go through the motions & who believe they are mere mortals. Their lives are as black & white as a 1950s television. Let's just say, it's not FUN.

And on the other side are Glitterati. For them, doors seem to effortlessly open. The Glitterati believe their lives to be be-witchingly beautiful, & so they are.

They live a kaleidoscope of rainbow colors & glitter, that would make Glinda from the *Wizard of Oz* smile in appreciation.

Okay, circle of truth time, in our heart of hearts, we all want to be Magical. We all want to walk into a room & have it light up because of our razzle dazzlenness. We all want people to stop us on the street & tell us we have the most beautiful smile (something that's happened to both Miss Kitty Kat & Pinup Julia on a weekly basis). We all want unbelievable business opportunities flooding into our inbox. We all want Romance with a capital R where the sky's the limit on the experiences you can adventure on with your (almost) perfect Sweetie. It's just the plain simple truth—we want the fairy tale, & we deserve it. So, if you want to be a Glitterati witch more than a humdrum Drabster, heed our Woo-Woo Showgirl advice!

Now rule number one for any witch is that you must believe you are Magical before you can be Magical. If you don't believe you're special, then you won't be able to cast those spells that give you The Universe on a plate.

Think of beauty as a mirror & you're the person smiling at it. When we look at ourselves in the mirror & the reflection isn't smiling back at us, we don't yell or blame the mirror for not giving us the results we want. Instead, we start smiling internally, which bubbles over to our mouth, so when we look in the mirror what do we see? A beautiful smiling person in front of us.

There are two ways to look at the world: through yourself & through everything other than yourself. We recommend the first way & here's why: it's a position of power.

And believe us, we ALL want to be powerful females.

Now maybe you have an issue with the word power. Perhaps it bothers you because you feel it is not right for you or females, in general, to be powerful. Or maybe some taught you that "power corrupts." Well, that's just Poppycock! Just because power is misused in the world does not mean it will corrupt you. And here's the thing, until you step up to the plate, claim your power, & own the fact that it's yours with all your heart, you will never be in control of your own life.

Women might be tender creatures, but within that softness is housed the power of an unconquerable Amazonian Queen (Hello, Wonder Woman!). For when you (not the outside world) define your beauty, everything else is filtered through that inner truth.

Conversely when you decide that the outside world will tell you whether or not you're beautiful, successful, smart, or confident, then you'll always be looking outside yourself for the answer. It's a system in which you're playing the game from a position of fear. All our thoughts & moves are in anticipation of how others will react, & as a result, we feel this intense need to control things. And the moment you try to control, you're blocking The Universe from working its Magic.

Now how do you know you're doing it right? Look to see how the world around you is treating you. Don't think of it as your definition of who you are but rather an energetic report card. If the world is treating you like you're the sassy, confident, Magical woman we know you are, then you get an A. But if you're not happy with what the world is mirroring back, then you need to hit the spell books!

And let's talk about losing the power of beauty. When you define your beauty based on some part of your body, such as your sexy legs, gorgeous red hair, or flawless skin, you have the ability to lose your beauty when you get a job where you sit at a desk all day long, you start to get gray hair, or those pesky little crow's feet come in. The power to create your own beauty means you'll never be chasing after something.

The Burlesque Hall of Fame Weekend in Las Vegas is one of the largest Burlesque festivals in the world. It is a fundraiser for the non-profit The Burlesque Hall of Fame, the only museum dedicated to the art of Burlesque. It's a spectacular event to see the best that the globe has to offer in the world of Burlesque.

Every year, the Friday night lineup honors the Burlesque Legends, our stars of yesteryear, with the annual Titans of Tease performance. These women, in their sixties, seventies, eighties, & nineties, remove their clothes & shimmy in style. Embracing their bodies, both past & present to standing ovations.

During the 2015 Burlesque Hall of Fame (BHoF) festival, Workin' The Tease was lucky enough to interview some of these legends for the documentary portion of our internet channel. In our "Why I Love Burlesque" episode, the eighty-four-year-old Dee Milo matter-of-factly stated that the reason she loved Burlesque was because, "Burlesque allows a human being to love the skin that they're in."

We're not saying don't go to the gym, dye your hair, or moisturize your skin; just know that you are truly moving from a position of power, & you are doing those beauty regimes for you & not for other people.

We're giving you the keys to the metaphysical kingdom, to beauty, for your entire life versus the fleeting moments of youth. Which means your only limitations are the ones you set up in your mind.

But we know you are ready for this; you picked up this book!

So stop living a Drabster life. Instead, raise your champagne flute to the beautiful people, because guess what, you're one of them!

***

Journal Prompt #2

What is your most beautiful part?

What are three things you do to make yourself feel beautiful every day?

If you aren't doing at least three things daily, why?

Now draw yourself as the most fabulous version you can imagine.

(It's not about being Picasso; drawing is a great way to tap into the part of your brain that knows more than our conscious mind can hold.)

AFFIRMATION

I am beautiful & I attract beautiful things.

(Say this in the mirror until the phrase makes you smile)

CONFIDENCE by Crystal Jernigan

2 - HAPPY IS AS HAPPY DOES

Happiness is the best makeup.

—*Drew Barrymore*

Most folks are about as happy as they make up their minds to be. Might as well be you!

So many people tell themselves a story where their happiness is contingent on something else. On winning an award, or finding the perfect Sweetie, or hitting a certain number in their bank account. But none of those things will make you truly happy. Yes, they might make you happy for a moment, but sooner than later, you find yourself longing for the next thing that will *finally* make you happy. Quite a vicious cycle that conditional thinking. . .

Trust the timing of your life. It's all working out perfectly. Enjoy the ride.

And the more you enjoy the ride, the more people will enjoy watching you. Happiness is like a magnet that attracts positivity. When we are on stage, the number one thing we hear is, "I love watching you—You look like you are having so much FUN."

Yup, that's right—the reason people like watching us isn't because of our nice tits or beautiful faces—it is because we look so happy on stage. The old Showgirl saying is true, "the more FUN you are having on stage, the more FUN the audience will have." And this same philosophy applies to life—the more FUN you are having in life, the more FUN will be attracted to you.

Real happiness is 100 percent unconditional. It is not based on anything external reality. Seriously, happiness just is.

It's just that simple.

***

Journal Prompt #3

Make a list of simple pleasures that bring you the feeling of happiness. Examples for us are walks in nature, listening to good music while cooking or playing with our dog. Once you have this list, pull it out anytime you need a way to tap into that happy spirit.

AFFIRMATION

Happiness is my default.

(Say this in the mirror until the phrase makes you smile)

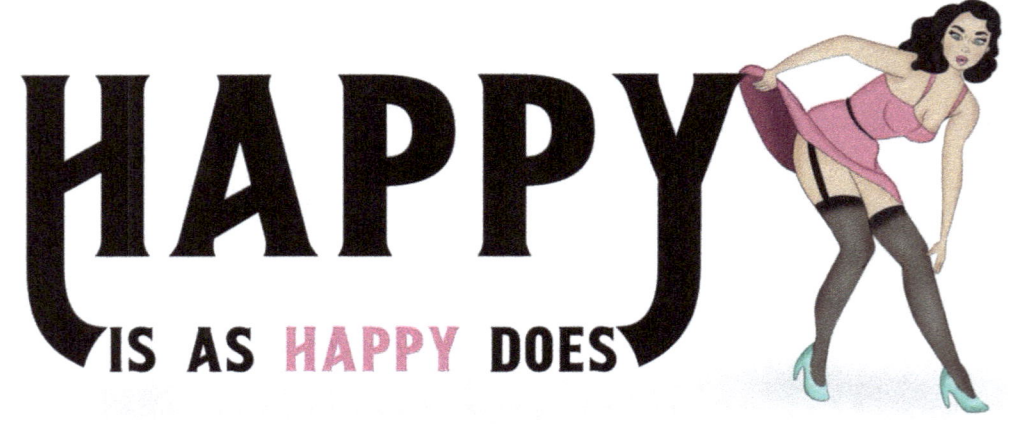

HAPPY by Amber Schindler

3 - YOU BEING YOU IS A GIFT

I've had to go against all kinds of people through the years just to be myself. I think everybody should just be allowed to be who they are.

—Dolly Parton

You might have also already heard this one: You are enough.

SERIOUSLY. YOU. ARE. ENOUGH!

Own the power of who you are & make sure to share it with other people.

There is something about you that is special. So special that it makes you "you"! Doing what you love is the cornerstone to this. Figure out what makes your heart sing & start doing it, because the moment you start doing this, you will sparkle & shine like the member of the Glitterati you were meant to be. We guarantee that if an idea is in you, it is for you. Follow your intuition & inspiration.

Individuality is your strongest of moves so make it bold. Self-awareness is sexy. Knowing your body & mind inside & out. Knowing you means you know what makes you look good.

Perfection is a joke that we forgot we were all in on (just like being normal. . .) So forget both concepts & just do you girlfriend! Think of yourself as Tinkerbell, so spread your pixie dust wherever you go.

Old Hollywood's sex symbol Mae West's film career began in 1932 at the age of thirty-nine.

Thirty-nine!

A vaudeville performer, she introduced the shimmy to the Broadway stage, something very scandalous in its day! Also a writer, West penned plays including the sold-out sensation SEX for which she was arrested. She was sentenced to ten days but was released one day early for good behavior.

For silver screen debut, West was hired for what was considered a bit part in a movie called *Night After Night*. Now Mae West was not a girl to be relegated to a

Drabster storyline. Quite unhappy with the role on the page, she insisted she be given power to rewrite all her dialogue with her fabulous wit.

COAT CHECK GIRL: Goodness! What lovely diamonds!

MAE WEST: Goodness had nothing to do with it.

As a result, Miss West stole the show in every scene even though the film was originally a vehicle for a guy named George Raft (Who's George Raft? Exactly!). He later said of their movie experience that, "she stole everything but the cameras." Now that's a lady comfortable with wielding power!

West was one of a kind & was honored for embracing who she was. As she stated, "I freely chose the life I led because I was convinced that a woman has as much right as a man to live the way she does if she does no actual harm to society."

This girl knew who she was & reveled in every moment of it. At one point in her career, Mae West was Hollywood's highest paid star. Her popularity had raised enough capital to save the failing & debt-ridden Paramount Pictures from bankruptcy. By the time she retired from the silver screen, Mae West had made nine movies, five of which she had writer's credit for.

Mae said it best, "Personality is glitter that sends your little gleam across the footlights & the orchestra pit into that black space where the audience is." And to the West, the entire world was her audience. She knew she was a gift & chose to share it with the world.

So how do you spread the gift of you? One of the simplest ways to do this is with the practice of nonjudgment.

We as human beings are constantly trying to label things as good or bad, but those are just labels. Human beings love labels: it feels so good to say that this situation is this & then put it in a little box. But the moment you stop labeling things & simply let it be, whether in your own life or anyone else's, is the moment you can truly live in the moment & allow life to happen to you.

There are many people in our lives who can't believe we take off our clothes in front of perfect strangers for money. Whether or not you think we're dirty Strippers, that's okay because we've come to terms with what we love doing. We love entertaining people, we love helping people, & we love inspiring people to have confidence & love their bodies inside & out.

By the way, we believe as a whole that Americans are waaaaaay too prudish when it comes to our bodies. Spend even a little time on a European beach & you'll see a lot of boobies, but here in America, you show a little boobage at the Big Game & what you'll get is millions of dollars in fines. We all have bodies. We have clitorises. We have vaginas. We have anuses. These are all gifts (yep, just as Alan Ginsberg noted in his poem "Howl," even the anus). Love them, embrace them, share them.

You have been criticizing yourself for years, & it hasn't worked. Try approving of yourself & see what Magic happens.

***

Journal Prompt #4

What women do you find Sexy? Dita Von Teese? Dolly Parton? Michelle Obama? Your Mom? It doesn't matter who it is—pick a few women you are naturally drawn to & write down the qualities that you love in them.

What you love in others, you can find in yourself. Acknowledging the traits you want to foster is a great first step, & we guarantee being perfect isn't on the list of what you love about these women. It is what makes them unique that makes them unforgettable.

AFFIRMATION

I am loved & I get to love.

(Say this in the mirror until the phrase makes you smile)

MAE WEST by Katie Kleinbaum

4 - IT'S OKAY TO SPARKLE

Well-behaved women seldom make history.

—*Laurel Thatcher Ulrich*

So, we have to take a moment to remind you that it's okay to sparkle. It's okay to stand out. It's okay if people want to look at you. Why wouldn't they want to look at you? You are beautiful, dammit!

But sometimes, we've been taught that it's not okay to sparkle. Maybe our mother, or our father, or our church, or our classmate, or our Shitty ex-boyfriend, or our Shitty ex-girlfriend taught us a Drabster tale.

And we believed them.

And then we caught a case of the Drabbies.

Perhaps we started to believe that we shouldn't be pretty because it made other people feel bad, so we dressed ourselves down. Or maybe we believed the people treating us special was a bad thing because it gave us an unfair advantage that not everyone got.

Girl, why are you trying so hard to fit in when you were born to stand out?

We're here to tell you to forget all that because: IT'S OKAY TO SPARKLE!!! IT'S OKAY TO SHINE!!! And this goes mentally, spiritually, emotionally, & physically.

Sparkle in your personality, sparkle in your wit, sparkle in your looks!

No one is born timid. Have you met a little kid? They are brash, cocky little Shits, & we mean that with the utmost respect! They do things for themselves & no one else.

When we're timid, we're actually playing a role, wearing a mask, being the person who we think people will like. Which probably means we're more worried/obsessed about what other people think of us. Total recipe for disaster because it's not honest. Stop hating yourself for everything you aren't, & start loving yourself for everything you are.

So now that we've cleared the air when it comes to being okay with sparkling, feel free to use the tools of being a female: hair flowers, sparkle bling, lipstick, false eyelashes, hair curlers, & high heels to do so. And this is true whether you're a physical female or have feminine energy.

When we're at a cocktail party & we meet a female who tells us how they love the costumes, makeup, & hairstyles of our fantastic over-the-top lifestyle, we always counter that they can embrace any & all aspects of our over-the-top lifestyle. But so many of them take another sip of their Chardonnay, look distantly out into the crowd, & counter with, "Oh, I could never do that."

Sure, you can, & it's just as easy as allowing yourself to shine a little bit more. Whether it be applying false eyelashes before you go out, sliding a hair flower behind your ear, or slipping into that sparkly dress you bought, but have never worn.

When you attend BHoF, one of the rites of passage as a Burlesque Dancer is to go to Du Barry Fashions & get a customized Rhinestone Name Necklace that serves as the de facto BHoF nametag.

We cannot convey this enough; there is nothing, absolutely nothing, understated about these rhinestone dog tags. These necklaces scream: Here I am, world, in all my sparkly glory!

Now, there are many nice reasons to have your name sparkle on your chest. First, it helps show off your boobies, something as women we should always be game for (God gave them to you for a reason). Second, it allows people to always remember your name. Seriously! Whenever we're somewhere new where you're meeting a lot of new people, like the first day of pole class, a Burlesque conference, &/or Burning Man, it's a fantastic gift to give the people you meet so that they don't have to worry about remembering your name. And you want the world to know your name!

At Du Barry Fashions, a Rhinestone Name Necklace with your name on it costs five dollars. Five dollars! That's less than Miss Kitty Kat spends on her single-origin light-roast pour-over coffee most of the time! Most hair flowers will run you a couple of dollars. But the results of wearing these elements of bling that help remind us to sparkle & shine is priceless.

So write your name in rhinestones, Girl, because you are a Star!

***

Journal Prompt #5

What did you enjoy doing & wearing when you were a kid? Can you find elements of that playfulness in your life today? If not, where can you add it in?

AFFIRMATION

It is good to do things that bring me joy.

(Say this in the mirror until the phrase makes you smile)

Pictures of Julia Reed Nichols & Kitty Kat DeMille as Kids

5 - KNOW YOUR WORTH, THEN ADD TAX

Keep your heels, head, & standards high.

—Coco Chanel

Knowing your self-worth & standing up for what you deserve have been severely undervalued, especially by the fairer sex.

During Miss Kitty Kat's time dancing in strip clubs, "Know Your Worth" was the ultimate Stripper mantra. This dancer's call to arms was uttered in many a locker room pep talk before heading out to the floor for the night.

But first, let's clarify the essence of this statement: knowing your worth means that in any given situation, you feel that you are an equal with anyone you interact with: clients, bosses, colleagues, or friends. And because of this feeling of power & control, you're willing to ask for what you want, plus tax.

Knowing your worth means you realize how much potential you have. That you are aware of your awesome qualities. That you start making positive changes toward what you want. Most importantly, you believe in yourself & don't let anyone tell you otherwise. And nowhere is this principle displayed better than in a strip club.

The funny thing about strip clubs, often "the prettiest" girl doesn't always make the most money. Instead, it's the girl with the most confidence. The girl who demands what she wants & then gets it, almost like magic (Wink, Wink). You might be a gorgeous six-feet-tall model type, but if you don't believe you're the bee's knees, no one else will.

Strip clubs are about crafting the ultimate fantasy, one that's irresistible to its patrons, than asking to be compensated for creating such a vision. Perhaps the question you should ask yourself is: Are you a twenty-dollar lap dancer on the floor or an $800-an-hour VIP type of gal? Because in the end, you can't out-earn your self-esteem level.

One night when Miss Kitty Kat was dancing at one of Las Vegas' massive strip clubs, one of the dancers there received a $20,000 tip. And on a Tuesday night to boot! Now this dancer only received that tip because she believed she deserved that tip. Hell, she probably demanded it, & the client was more than willing to oblige. That Dancer knew what she was worth, & because she asked, The Universe provided.

If perhaps you counter with, "Oh, that's not me," just remember that she who argues for her limitations gets to keep them.

If it still feels uncomfortable to you, maybe you should ask yourself if you have all the time in the world to lean into bad beliefs. If you do, feel free to carry on as usual, but if you want things to change, then you & your self-value might need to have a heart-to-heart.

✳✳✳

Journal Prompt #6

Make two columns. In Column 1, write down all the ways you undervalue yourself at home, work, school, or in relationships. Be honest with yourself. What resources are you giving away below what they are worth—time, money, & energy all count here. In Column 2, write down your true worth—the value you would tell your best friend they are worth for the same task. Notice if the two columns match, are close, or are very far apart.

AFFIRMATION

I am a luxury product.

(Say this in the mirror until the phrase makes you smile)

I AM by Kitty Kat DeMille

6 - STOP APOLOGIZING FOR YOUR CHOICES

When caught between two evils, I generally pick the one I've never tried before.

—*Mae West*

I always knew movement was my medium. It's always what I've done. Does a racehorse run? You bet like Hell they do. Well, Ophelia Flame Strips!

—*Ophelia Flame*

In order to love who you are, you cannot hate the experiences that shaped you. One of our most favorite interviews at BurlyCon 2014 was with Miss Ophelia Flame, pioneer of the Minneapolis neo-Burlesque scene, a founder of Lili's Burlesque Revue, & an all-around mover & shaker in the world of Burlesque. Known as "The Burning Sensation," Ophelia was the first runner-up for the Reigning Queen of Burlesque 2012, has competed at the BHoF more times than we can count, & has been nominated as one of the top fifty Burlesque performers in the world by the *21st Century Burlesque* magazine.

"One thing I learned being a Stripper, which is just as important in life, is that people are as judgmental as you are apologetic. Whether it's Stripping, Burlesque, or anything else people might have conflict with."

<u>Read that again—people are as judgmental as you are apologetic.</u>

Ophelia never apologized for her life's choices; she never made excuses. "I was a Stripper for ten years, I traveled the world, I made a Shit ton of money, & it allowed me to do many things that I might not have done otherwise." Because she owned who she was, people usually responded with the statement, "Huh, interesting, so what do you want for dinner? Steak or chicken?"

The crazy thing is most of the beliefs you harbor inside of your brain are not actually yours, but were put there by someone else—your parents, your religion, your society. So many times, when we become adults, we keep believing these outdated concepts because it's all we've known, instead of looking down deep inside of us, & deciding who we want to be.

DON'T BE A BELIEF THIEF!

When Ophelia announced to her feminist mother that she had decided to become a Stripper, there were definitely some protests. "I told her, 'I love you & I know you're concerned, but I will do you everything to allow you to feel like I'm safe.'" So Ophelia invited her mom to her Strip Club to see where she was building her career. "She came one night & saw my locker & met the bouncer, the DJ, & the House Mom."

And at the end of the night, Ophelia's Mama said she was fine with Ophelia's choice. But she included one requirement, "If you're gonna be a Stripper, you better be the best goddam Stripper out there."

Ophelia did her best to comply.

***

Journal Prompt #7

Are there parts of your life that you are hiding? If not, do you secretly have lifestyles that interest you? Have a great business idea? Want to play with BDSM? Want to start a blog? Give yourself the permission to explore the idea on paper—sometimes, the process of writing it down is enough, & sometimes, it is the first step in a very FUN process of creation!

AFFIRMATION

The things I love lift me up.

(Say this in the mirror until the phrase makes you smile)

LIFE IS THE BUBBLES by Kitty Kat DeMille

BODY LOVE

7 - BE YOUR OWN GREATEST LOVER

Abundance is not something we acquire. It is something we tune into.

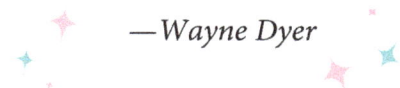

—*Wayne Dyer*

Stop sitting around for someone to show up & give you permission to do the stuff you really want to do. Just Fucking do it! Self-love is the greatest middle finger to waiting for Prince Charming!

If you love flowers & want your Sweetie to buy them, stop that waiting & buy them for yourself, because you deserve them. If you love dancing, treat yourself to classes. Buy those shoes that make you feel special. Go to that concert you've always wanted to go to even if no one else wants to go. The funny thing is usually the moment you start doing these things for yourself, other people will start doing it for you.

The reason is because these things raise what we in the Woo-Woo community call your "vibrational frequency." Here's the skinny—your body is composed of energy-producing particles, each of which is in constant motion. And depending on how fast these particles move determines your frequency, which ultimately determines what you attract.

So, like everything & everyone else in The Universe, you are vibrating & creating energy. Take responsibility for the energy you create & give yourself the gift of "high vibe" experiences.

Take yourself out on dates. Schedule them in your planner & make sure not to break them for something "more important." If you can't find the time to treat yourself right, how can you expect someone else to? Your job is to make you your Number One Priority.

Make self-contentment & independence an art form. You are the only one who is going to make you happy, so you better get going at making sure you are!

***

Journal Prompt #8

Make a list of three things you can do every day to raise your vibrational frequency. Mediation? Painting Your Nails? A Spin Class? Now that you have those things, write them on your calendar for the next week. Stick to your plan & notice what happens. We promise, life will feel lighter, & you'll start manifesting all kinds of Magic.

AFFIRMATION

Taking time for me makes me more productive & abundant.

(Say this in the mirror until the phrase makes you smile)

SELF CARE by Lora Merhi

8 - WORDS HAVE MAGIC, THAT'S WHY IT'S CALLED SPELLING

> Don't speak negatively about yourself, even as a joke.
> Your body doesn't know the difference.
> Words are energy & cast spells, that's why it's called spelling.
>
> —*Bruce Lee*

Words have so much power, & we don't even realize it.

Words create our lives, our reality, our Universe. They truly are Magical!

Without them, a thought can never become a reality. Words are energy that actually cast spells; that's why it's called SPELLING.

Words are made up of vibration translated through sound. It is these vibrations that are the building blocks of the reality that surrounds us.

A self-fulfilling prophecy is a phenomenon of someone predicting (or expecting) something & this prediction (or expectation) coming true simply because the person believes it will. Our words are a confirmation to the world of how we see ourselves, others, & our lives. So choose your words carefully!

We can choose to use this force constructively with words of encouragement, or destructively use words of despair. With them, we are bestowed the ability to heal, to help, to hurt, to hinder, to humiliate, to humble, & to harm.

Be sure to taste your words before you spit them out. Choosing different words gives you the ability to transform not only your life but also the lives of others.

In the first few years Pinup Julia & Kitty Kat met each other, the gals would spend copious amounts of time talking about the future. How one day, they would tour the country doing good by performing Burlesque, entertaining thousands of people, & attending some of the most lavish parties. Flash forward almost a decade later & those dreams are a reality.

- Julia founded Do Right Industries—A company dedicated to creating entertainment with purpose, which has employed over 103 different artists in forty-seven states to create projects that positively impact their local communities with art. Additionally, Do Right's heartfelt & glitzy work has been seen on The Game Show Network, The Hallmark

Channel, The Huffington Post, NBC, ABC, Fox, & numerous other outlets across the world.

- Julia & Kat created Workin' The Tease, which focuses on self-empowerment by showing off what's underneath! This brand has performed in a total of eight states. WTT Burly's #StripForPP fundraisers for Planned Parenthood have been held in both Los Angeles (four times) & Portland (two times). They have donated close to twenty thousand dollars between funds raised & donated tickets to Planned Parenthood employees. To top that, the Burlesque channel featuring all things beautiful, body positive, & Burly has produced over 200 videos with a combined total of two million views on YouTube & Facebook.

- Julia created Pin-Ups on Tour, a World War Two–style vintage variety Burlesque show. This brand has performed in forty-six states, donated over 4,000 tickets back to our military heroes, & has been able to entertain close to 3,500 Active Duty & Veteran Service Members in the nation's VA Hospitals! In these past few years, they have donated over $70,000 in free veteran tickets & monetary donations to nonprofits such as AmVets, Heels for Combat Boots, Recon Sniper Foundation, Pin-Ups for Vets, American Legion posts, Grow For Vets, & VFW posts.

- Pinup Julia & Kitty Kat created The Green Light District, the Las Vegas & Los Angeles–based Event & Entertainment Group for the Cannabis Connoisseur. They were the featured entertainment at parties for MJBizCon Week in Las Vegas, NV, Dope Cup High Desert in Adelanto, CA, the Cannabis Cup in Sacramento & Riverside, CA.

- Pinup Julia created The Event People, a creative co-op of experienced professionals dedicated to creating unique marketing experiences, entertainment, & events. This creative community allows clients to connect directly with artists to achieve out-of-this world results. Their Space, The Drawing Room, is housed in the heart of the arts district in Las Vegas—so pop in & say "hi" if you see them there!

- And most recently, both Julia & Kat helped create The Drawing Room Foundation, a 501(c)3 that is dedicated to creating community through art. They currently serve on the board of directors—where they get to encourage art, entrepreneurship, local business & community betterment across America.

All this from two gals who used to sit in Julia's one-bedroom apartment in Santa Monica talking of things to come, using their imagination to spell out the future.

***

Journal Prompt #9

Write a letter to your future self—Congratulating yourself for something you currently want to accomplish. Write this letter as if you have ALREADY ACCOMPLISHED what you want. Write the letter as if it has already happened & you are enjoying all the amazing material & emotional rewards of your success. This is a great exercise to help your brain & words catch up to the truth—you can have what you want RIGHT NOW.

AFFIRMATION

It feels good to get what I want.

(Say this in a mirror until the phrase makes you smile)

Words To Keep it In the Past ....

I felt <u>EMOTION</u> when <u>EVENT HAPPENED.</u>
Example: I felt SUPPORTED when MY SHOW SOLD OUT.

I said <u>YES/NO</u> when I was offered <u>WHAT.</u>
Example: I said yes when I was offered my dream job
Example: I said no when I was offered another date with my ex

The unexpected brought me joy today.

9 - STRIKE A POWER POSE...THERE'S NOTHING TO IT

Don't fake it till you make it. Fake it till you become.

- Amy Cuddy

In our grandmother's day, finishing schools would make their young ladies walk around with a book on their head. Good posture was considered a sign of good etiquette. Turns out it probably made our Nanas happier & powerful too, & a couple of generations later, we know why.

We all know that your emotions are reflected in your physical state. Your posture is different when you're happy, as opposed to when you're sad. But you might not know that the inverse actually works too! Your physical state can actually alter your emotions. Your body language sends signals to your brain about how you're feeling & operating, & your brain believes them to be true.

If you have poor posture, it tends to bring out poor emotions or a negative state. Alternatively, good posture can produce a more positive-centered state. Stand up & you'll feel prouder & alert, slump over & you'll feel more negative. So, if you want to change your mindset, the easiest of places to start is by changing your posture.

These theories were illuminated even more with Amy Cuddy's 2012 Ted Talk, "Your Body Language Shapes Who You Are." This speech became one of the most watched Ted Talks ever garnering sixty-one million views. According to Cuddy, a social psychologist at Harvard Business School, everyone should spend two minutes power posing.

What, you ask, is power posing? It is the act of adopting stances associated with confidence, power, & achievement, such as a lifted chest, head held high, & arms either up or propped on the hips. Cuddy has shown that how we hold our bodies, aka "postural feedback," can influence our emotional state, behavior, & self-assessments. How's that for Magic?

Both humans & animals express power through their bodies. When they feel on top of the world, they sprawl out becoming more open. It's similar to how primates behave in the wild. They puff out their chests & extend their limbs to make themselves appear & feel big.

Conversely, humans & primates tumble in on themselves when they feel unsure, making themselves smaller by hunching over, crossing their arms over their chest, & avoiding big movements. "Our nonverbals govern how we think & feel about ourselves. Our bodies change our minds," stated Cuddy.

This led to Cuddy creating specific power poses that open up the body. According to Cuddy's initial research (which to this day is considered controversial), after assuming a high-power pose for just two minutes, your testosterone levels (the "dominance" hormone) can rocket 20 percent, while your cortisol levels (the "stress" hormone) fall sharply, thus allowing you to better handle stressful situations.

FIVE KICKASS POWER POSES TO STRIKE

- **Wonder Woman:** It's the classic crime-fighter pose! Plant your fleet hips-width apart, put your hands on your hips, push out your chest, & tilt your chin upward. This pose conveys confidence & power, even if you're feeling nervous. Angling your chin upward is the opposite of touching your neck or ducking your head, which are signs of both anxiety & submission.

- **The CEO:** Named after Oprah Winfrey because of the way she sits: leaning back, at ease, with her arms behind her head. "This body language naturally projects dominance," explains Cuddy. "It's unusual to see a woman in this position." There are multiple variations of this pose (crossing your knees or resting your ankle on your knee), but the key is to relax back into your chair with your hands behind your head.

- **The Performer:** And the crowd goes wild! This power pose, named after Mick Jagger of the Rolling Stones, involves throwing both your hands in the air & standing with your feet wide apart. "This is a classic expression of feeling powerful in the moment," explains Cuddy, "It causes you to physically expand."

- **The Loomer:** This pose is named after former American President Lyndon B. Johnson, who at six feet four inches hovered over most people. Cuddy noted how "he used his stature very thoughtfully, to both intimidate & seduce." To utilize this pose, plant your hands on the table & lean forward. Leaning forward while standing shows you're engaged & in a position of dominance. You will seem taller & more authoritative, particularly during presentations or pitches.

- **The Obama:** Cuddy named this power pose after the forty-fourth President because he often sat like this while in the Oval Office. The pose expresses power & dominance. It involves resting your feet on the table while clasping your hands behind your head as you lean back. It can be a bit tricky to execute so it requires some practice, but when done right, your co-workers will definitely be humming Hail to the Chief around your desk!

So next time you find yourself in a bad mood, take a deep breath, roll your shoulders back, & do the Wonder Woman for two minutes. Tiara & Lasso of Truth are optional!

***

Journal Prompt #10

Let's give this a try! First - give yourself a temperature check. How do you feel physically, emotionally, & spiritually at this very moment?

Now - pick your favorite pose & give it a try for two minutes. Now - how do you feel? How did this physical experience affect your emotions?

AFFIRMATION

It feels good to strike a pose.

(Say this in a mirror until the phrase makes you smile)

WOMAN by Amber Schindler

10 - SHAKE THAT ASS

Good ideas originate in the muscles.

—Thomas Edison

Since this book is written by two Burlesque Dancers, you shouldn't be surprised that we're gonna tell you to shake that ass...

Now there're a thousand reasons (& books about it) why exercise is good for us physically, but we're here to talk about the reasons you should incorporate movement into your life spiritually.

Movement is a gateway to experiencing the full range of your spiritual connection. Your mind & your body are as much dance partners as much as Fred & Ginger were. Your body is a reflection of your mind, as your mind is a reflection of your body.

Movement truly allows you to drop in a Flow State aka "being in The Zone." Flow State is when you are fully present in the moment. This results in a feeling of energized focus, full involvement, & enjoyment in the process of the activity.

Essentially, a Flow State is characterized by complete absorption in what one does.

In other words, you are just being.

People tend to think of spirituality as sitting quietly on a bougie Anthropologie pillow & meditating. But physicality can be just as meditative as stillness.

Think back to your high school art class days to the world of clay sculpture. To start to create something, you would need to grab some clay from the bucket. Now this clay had not moved in quite some time. Truthfully until that moment, that clay had just sat there day in & day out.

But because you wanted to create the next Venus de Milo, you needed to work the clay. You needed to mold & form it into the look you wanted. And the more you bend & stretched the clay, the easier it became to use! This is true about both your body & your mind. The more you move your body, the more it will translate to every other part of your life.

If your body is stiff & rigid, usually your mind is stiff & rigid, & vice versa. Thus, when you start to stretch your body, & lo & behold, your mind will also begin to stretch.

When you are trying to make changes in your life, it behooves you to include movement on this journey. Because in motion, we can transmute the traumas of our past. Sometimes, the only way to process the more toxic parts of yourself, such as anger, grief, & shame, is to move & allow yourself to really experience the full spectrum of your feelings.

But not all motions are created equal. Different kinds of physicality bring out different feelings within us.

Below are some different categories of exercise & how that can help different spiritual aspects of our lives. Just realize that many movements can fit into more than one spiritual classification. Intention plays a big role in the world of motion (really, in everything in life). Just know that if you're attracted to a certain type of movement, there's a reason why.

- **EMOTIONAL PROCESSING MOVEMENTS**

- Kickboxing
- Boxing
- Drumming Workouts
- Hitting a Pillow

- **REPETITIVE MOVEMENTS (PERFECT FOR AFFIRMATION STATEMENTS)**
  - Swimming
  - Running
  - Biking
  - Rowing

- **JOYOUS MOVEMENTS**
  - Aerobics
  - Pole Dancing

- Zumba
- Salsa Dancing
- Jumping on a Trampoline
- Hula Hooping

- **REFLECTIVE MOVEMENTS**
  - Yoga
  - Tai Chi
  - Meditative Walking
  - Ballet

When all else fails, you can always focus on your breath. That's where it all starts & ends.

***

Journal Prompt #11

Today's prompt is to get you out of your head & into your body. First, check in with yourself. How do you physically feel? How are your emotional vibrations at this moment & what thoughts are dominating your mind? Now, pick one of the activities listed in this book & DO IT! (Hint: pick the one that sounds FUN!) Finally, check-in again—compared to before, you moved—how are your physical health, emotional vibration, mental clarity, & stream of thoughts?

AFFIRMATION

My body & my mind communicate clearly to support my health.

(Say this in a mirror until the phrase makes you smile)

YOGA by Lora Merhi

11 - PLAY DRESS UP WITH YOUR LIFE

I live by a man's code, designed to fit a man's world, yet at the same time I never forget that a woman's first job is to choose the right shade of lipstick.

—*Carole Lombard*

One of our favorite things about Burlesque is that you're given the leeway to be different characters at different times. In one act, you can be the sweet Girl-Next-Door, & in the following, you can be the Tawdry-Temptress.

Both of those aspects exist in your personality, so embrace them.

Life is about experiences, which means you never have to settle for Plain Vanilla (Unless you want Vanilla because there are times we absolutely love Vanilla!)

As children, we loved to play pretend, we loved to play make-believe. And it still rings true, no matter the age! Embrace these characters in your clothes, hairstyle, even your undergarments!

Give yourself permission to be a mixture of Sunshine & Hurricane. It is oppressive always having to act the same, to play the same boring mundane role that work, family, & duty impose on us. We all want the chance to be different. We want to be the perky punkette & the epitome of old-fashioned vintage glamor.

But remember, everyone is a public performer. We are always acting, we're always playing a role. But Drabsters have cast themselves in bit parts in their own lives.

But not you, you are one of the Magical Glitterati, which gives you permission to play the role of a Leading Lady. And Darling, we cannot say this enough, your stage awaits you!

Think About Who You Choose To Be When You Put On:

- **Bras** (Lacey Push-Up, Vinyl Bustier, Pastel Bralette, Bedazzled Corset, No Bra)
- **Panties** (Black High Waisted, White Cotton, Lacey Thong, Garter Belt)
- **Dresses** (Wiggle Dress, Cocktail Dress, Flapper Dress, Swing Dress)

- **Tops** (Classic White T-Shirt, Peasant Blouse, Argyle Sweater, Button-Up Cardigan)

- **Skirts** (Micro Mini, Prep School Plaid Kilt, Knee Length Tennis, Tea Length A-Line, Flowy Bohemian Maxi Skirt)

- **Bottoms** (Kickass Power suit, Black Leather Pants, Timeless Jeans, Romper)

- **Fancy Dresses** (Little Black Dress, Sequins, Cocktail)

- **Shoes** (Five-Inch Pleasers, Chunky Wedges, Fuzzy Slippers, Rhinestone Slingbacks, Open-Toed Mules)

- **Jewelry** (Rhinestone Name Necklace, Bangle Bracelets, Diamond Earrings, Black Leather Choker)

- **Hair Accessories** (Red Hair Flower, Black Fascinator, Pom Pom Knit Cap, Sparkly Tiara, Beanie Hat)

- **Jackets & Coats** (Lace Bolero, Black Leather Jacket, Trench coat, Jean Jacket, Red Pea Coat)

- **Sleepwear Lingerie** (Playful Babydoll, Embroidered Lace Teddy Bodysuit, Satin Robe, Contrasting Piping PJ Set)

Each of these wardrobe choices is a choice on your personality for the day. There's even a scientific term for it: "Enclothed Cognition." That's just a fancy way of saying that clothing affects how we think. The theory says that the clothing we wear (or that others wear) actually changes our thought patterns.

When we interviewed Los Angeles Burlesque teacher Vixen DeVille for our podcast *Better Than Sex*, she explained it perfectly! "Your Burlesque should be whatever is missing from your real life." When Vixen first started in the world of Burlesque, all her characters were powerful femme fatale characters such as the Snow Queen, Maleficent, & a Fire Demon. "This was because in real life I was very much a 'Yes' person. I wasn't very confident in my own opinions & tastes. I was always trying to fit in all the time. So I wanted to go on stage & feel powerful & in control & not give a Shit." So she dressed up as an all-powerful Ice Queen covered in bedazzled white rhinestones & a dangerously high slit.

Clothing is a form of self-expression. Each shoe choice, hair flower, or bra & panty set are clues to who it empowers you to play. We recommend doing this over buying bag costumes because you are able to customize your outfit while getting the added pleasure of creating, crafting, & Rhinestone-ing your costumes (we're telling you, your life hasn't started until you've started bedazzling stuff!)

But if you're still a bit unsure about stepping outside your door playing this new role, feel free to dress up as your new character in the comfort of your own home.

***

Journal Prompt #12

Draw your dream Burlesque costume. Allow yourself to be inspired—surf the Interwebs for inspiration. Think of what you'd want—Corset? Pasties? Thong? Fringe? Tassels? Rhinestones? Wigs? Allow yourself to become the Showgirl, Drag Queen, or Drag King of your dreams!

AFFIRMATION

More is more!

(Say this in the mirror until the phrase makes you smile)

BEAUTY IS BLIND by Emily Ford

12 - MOTHER NATURE IS YOUR BESTIE

The clearest way into The Universe is through a forest wilderness.

—John Muir

We thoroughly recommend wandering into the forest to lose your mind & find your soul.

Think back to when you were a kid. You probably spent a good amount of time picking daisies, lying in the grass, & staring at clouds lazily passing by, but sometimes as we get older, we lose those connections to the natural world.

We as performers love stage lights, audiences, & applause, but we also equally appreciate star lights, not a single other soul, & absolute silence. So wash your spirit clean with fresh air & sunshine because with every walk with nature, a gal receives more than she seeks.

Witchy gals believe that every living thing is made up of energy (aka vibrations). Which means that all these witches (aka powerful fierce female energy) have a spiritual connection to the elements of the Earth & the forces of nature.

Whether you have ten minutes or seven hours, find some time to be in nature every day. We feel that whenever we are feeling stuck or sad, spending some time in nature immediately makes us feel more refreshed & energized. The Earth is like an enormous battery, & when we connect with it, we recharge & create some much-needed inner peace.

Whenever we are on the road doing a longer tour with Pin-Ups on Tour, Workin' The Tease, or The Green Light District, we make sure to experience the natural wonders of this country. Julia, Kitty Kat, & oodles of our casts have explored Natural Hot Springs in Nevada, Colorado, & Utah. There's nothing like Spa Day, especially when it's in the Great Outdoors! This time disconnecting allows us to transform, awaken, heal, & find that boost of creativity we need to continue performing for audiences all over the country.

So wander where the WiFi is weak & embrace all the elements. Because as John Muir said, "of all the paths you take in life, make sure a few of them are dirt."

***

Journal Prompt #13

Where does your wanderlust take you? Craft a list of places in nature that you connect with, & then go there.

AFFIRMATION

I am one with nature.

(Say this in the mirror until the phrase makes you smile)

DOLLY by Amber Schindler

13 - SMOKE & MIRRORS ARE YOUR FRIENDS

If you're sad, add more lipstick & attack.

—Coco Chanel

Everyone thinks anyone who takes off their clothes for a living is perfect, but every Burlesque Dancer & Stripper knows that we all need a little help to look spectacular. People fall in love with your essence, not what you say or look like. But whatever makes you feel pretty is a gift because it helps you love yourself more.

Beauty products are there to inspire the inner goddess in you to greater heights. It helps you sparkle inside & out! Gods & Goddesses are created in our imagination, but they are brought to life with five-inch heels, push-up bras, mascara, & gobs of hairspray.

And any Burlesque Star can attest to the fact that makeup is definitely one of God's greatest gifts! From Pin-Up Styles to Vampy Vixens to Femme Fatales,

Burlesque is full of different hair & makeup looks. All that are artfully crafted not to make us feel pretty, but to make us feel powerful. Give us some glowing highlights, a poppin' lip gloss, & some kickass eyeliner, & we can do no wrong.

Makeup is self-confidence applied directly to the face. So thank your lucky stars that as women, we are able to wear it. If you're having a bad day, you can change that. Glamor is a state of mind.

Since Pinup Julia started Pin-Ups On Tour in 2015, we've done a multitude of pinup photo shoots with female veterans, military wives, & everyday women. And all we can say is there is nothing more Magically powerful than a makeover.

These females might not normally wear the copious amounts of hair spray & makeup products that we apply to their faces, but they sure reap the benefits of looking at themselves in the mirror. A few Victory Rolls & a tube of Kiss a Vet lipstick later, these women were ready to conquer the world in style.

Just like you. So grab your Magic mascara wand & spread that pixie dust on your face.

***

Journal Prompt #14

What would make you feel glamorous? Eye Lashes? Red Lipstick? A new pair of Heels? This is where you give yourself permission to treat yourself!

Now, we aren't advocating you spend money you don't have—but there are some great options at thrift stores & online. And sometimes, when you invest in yourself, it energetically gives others permission to invest in you as well.

AFFIRMATION

Investing in feeling beautiful is worth it!

(Say this in the mirror until the phrase makes you smile)

MIRROR by Amber Schindler

14 - BE NAKED MORE

> Most virtue is demand for great seduction.
>
> —*Natalie Barney*

Be Naked More!

Seriously, it will make you healthier! Little kids are completely comfortable being naked, & they never question whether or not they're happy. Coincidence? We think not! Being carefree about being stripped down to your bare essentials will allow you to be more comfortable wearing clothes, & taking them off.

Now the law says that when you're out in public, you need to be decent (sadly we are not writers of laws; otherwise, we'd repeal this silliness right away!), but there's nobody restricting you from being naked in your own home! So jump into the world of total freedom in your own personal castle!

Listen, we all have body issues, whether we're too skinny, too fat, our boobs are too small, too big, too saggy, or two different sizes. But the sooner we get over these issues, the sooner we get to have FUN!

When most people start out in the Burlesque world, they usually cover themselves up more than seasoned performers: wearing tights, higher cut panties, etc. But as a performer's self-confidence rises due to experience, so does the ability to be more okey-dokey in our birthday suits.

Clothes by nature are restrictive. They limit you from a full range of movement. They also can slow down or stop the flow of blood depending on how tight you wear your clothes. The tighter the clothes, the more they impede healthy blood flow. So if you're rocking that corset, a couple hours in your birthday suit is in order (luckily if you're rocking a corset, there's usually someone to help you in to your birthday suit. . .)

Biologically, nakedness is a sort of therapeutic massage for depression, low self-esteem, & other mental problems. Lying naked helps improve your blood flow, detoxifies your system, & thus provides you warmth & freedom. Sleeping nude allows the air to travel freely over your entire body. This allows your body to be able to distribute heat effectively so you'll be cooler in the summer & warmer in the winter. Other benefits include clothes lasting longer, no nasty stains on said clothes, skinny dipping is tons of FUN, & fertility is improved by being naked.

And MOST IMPORTANTLY, the more time you're comfortable being naked with yourself, the more comfortable you'll be naked when other people are around. Cause really that's when the FUN begins.

***

Journal Prompt #15

Stand in front of the mirror naked. Look at all parts of yourself. How does this make you feel? What emotions does this bring up? Can you find things to enjoy about the freedom of being naked? What can you find to love about your beautiful naked self? Have nice Tits? A great Ass? Beautiful Hair? Lovely Toes? Celebrate it all!

AFFIRMATION

I am beautiful.

(Say this in the mirror (naked this time) until the phrase makes you smile)

NAKED by Amber Schindler

15 - SILENCE IS SEXY

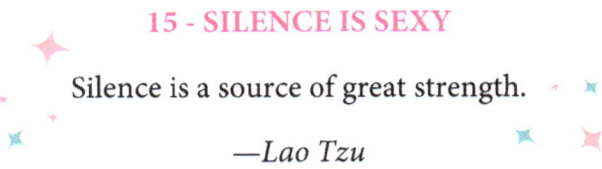

Silence is a source of great strength.

—*Lao Tzu*

Silence is a source of great strength. In silence, we can become aware of both ourselves & others. All this leads to being more mindful & self-compassionate in our lives.

And one of the easiest ways to do so is by not interrupting others. Also don't finish other people's sentences. Really, we can take this one back to grade school, just don't be rude!

Because the quieter you become, the more you can hear. By choosing silence, you will naturally listen more, allowing others the opportunity to share more, thus deepening your connection in the relationship.

When we interviewed Burlesque superstar Ophelia Flame, she had just taught a class at BurlyCon called Calm the Fuck Down. She explained that one of the number one telltale signs that a performer, or really anyone in general, is nervous & riddled with anxiety is their need to constantly talk.

"When you incessantly talk, you're breathing from your chest, versus your diaphragm. Which means you're positively exhausting yourself. I call it working yourself into a froth," notes Ophelia. "When we're babies, we breathe from our bellies, & then sooner or later, we all start breathing with our chests. But when we breath with our chests, it's slow, shallow, & short. Your brain isn't getting enough oxygen, your muscles aren't getting enough oxygen." For Ophelia, the solution to this nervous anxiety is to breathe. "Breathing diaphragmatically is the key."

Another tool that Ophelia recommended is meditation. Meditation is a great way to connect with your Higher Self. It eliminates worries, anxieties, & other negative emotions. And in lessening these lower frequencies, you can connect to your personal Magic. Meditation also helps you detach in a healthy way, & Detachment is Sexy (As Fuck!)

You are the creator of your own reality, which means you can set the vibrations for your body & mind. But to do so, you need to remember who you are, not who you are not. And one of the easiest ways to do this is to stop identifying with the outer world & to stop believing in the illusion.

As Rumi (a poet who lived in a world of words) stated, "the quieter you become, the more you are able to hear."

***

Journal Prompt #16

Where are the moments in your life that you can find more silence? What is one commitment you can make to add more silence in your life? Examples would be making an effort to interrupt less or dedicating five minutes a day to mediation.

AFFIRMATION

I celebrate the moments to be silent & listen.

(Say this in a mirror until the phrase makes you smile)

Behind The Scenes from Episode #2 of Workin' The Tease's podcast BETTER THAN SEX ft. Angel Beau

LIFE IMPROVEMENT

16 - OWN THE ROOM BEFORE YOU ENTER IT

A flower does not think of competing with the flower next to it.

It just blooms.

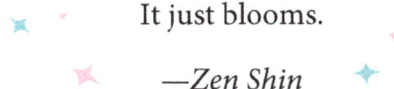

—*Zen Shin*

In the world of creating your own reality, intention has some atom bomb power! You can't live a positive life with a negative mind so you need to consistently believe that the next moment is going to be wonderfully Magical. This is something that Drabsters have forgotten while the Glitterati has a laser-like focus on.

Life comes to you based on where you're intending. If you're happy, The Universe will bring you happy experiences, & if you're sad, The Universe will bring you sad experiences. Either way, The Universe doesn't judge what you're asking for; it only gives you what you ask for.

Which means you should always own the room before you enter it. Drabsters hope the people on the other side of the proverbial door will love them, while the Glitterati know that those people will love them because they love themselves.

In other words, knowing is the name of the game; heck, it's the game itself.

So, the best thing you can do for yourself is intend what will come. To set a clear intention for what you want to experience to be. And don't only do this when walking into that proverbial door, but every door you encounter.

***

Journal Prompt #17

Think of the next door you know you are going to be walking through—Work, the gym, school, your house, the club—wherever. Close your eyes & get real clear about the picture. Once you can see it clearly, open your eyes & write a clear intention for that moment. The Magic will come when you simply notice the results, & the more you use this power, the more unstoppable you will become.

AFFIRMATION

This World Is My Bitch

(Say this phrase in the mirror until it makes you smile)

DOOR by Amber Schindler

17 - BE A KICKASS BACK UP DANCER

You have two hands. One to help yourself, the second to help others.

—*Audrey Hepburn*

Everyone likes being the star but being the backup dancer is equally as awesome.

Supporting others is one of the most important keys to succeeding in life. Seriously, life is not the competition we've been brought up to believe it is. Blowing out someone's birthday candles won't make yours shine brighter.

Be somebody who makes everyone feel like somebody. Build a strong support system through creating positive relationships & loyal friendships.

We totally acknowledge that it is not your job to make other people happy, but you can most definitely be their cheerleader when they succeed. Make the world a prettier place by sending out good vibrations. We were made to encourage each other along our journey, so why not be the reason someone smiles today!

And if someone isn't being the nicest person to you, give them the benefit of the doubt. Assume that they're going through a wobbly moment, give them some love, & you continue your Magical day. Showing respect to people who might not deserve it at that moment is not a reflection of their vibes, but of yours.

This is not to say you should tolerate those who do not see your value. Feel free to kick those people to the curb. Thank them for being part of your journey, how they helped you to grow & expand, & then head on your merry way! Remember, the loudest boos always come from the cheapest of seats.

***

Journal Prompt #18

Looking at your life—where are their opportunities to be a supporting player? How can you lift others up?

AFFIRMATION

We all rise together.

(Say this phrase in a mirror until it makes you smile)

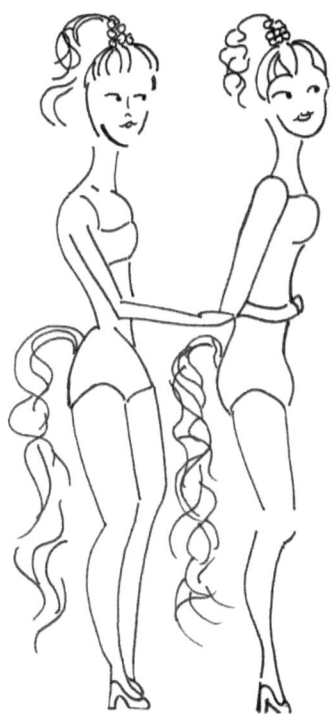

GIRL, WE'VE GOT THIS! by Kitty Kat DeMille

18 - DOING IT IN HEELS BACKWARD

> There's nothing damnable about being a strong woman. The world needs strong women.
>
> —*Ginger Rogers*

Empowered women empower women.

Ginger Rogers had to dance every move that Fred Astaire did in heels backward. And that's what made her Ginger Rogers, not Fred Astaire.

Yes, sometimes being a woman isn't the easiest of genders, but hey, what gender is? You're here for the experience so you should embrace it & the other women who support you.

Empowering women does not come from self-ish-ness but self-less-ness.

Helping another woman win, boosting her self-esteem, sharing a resource with her, complimenting her mind, body, & soul, & showing your appreciation, do not take away from your success as a Divine Magical Woman.

PLACES TO MEET YOUR NEXT BADASS BFF

- Fitness & Yoga Classes—We can't tell you how many bright souls we've connected with on our yoga mat.

- Try Something New—Want to Learn to Pole Dance? Or what about aerial circus arts? Or Fire? There are classes for everything & the likelihood that your classmates will be other fierce women is Super High!

- Business Networking Events—We go to chamber events, young business events, & industry networking mixers to connect with like-minded people who are also kickass women.

- Dating Apps—Yup, the same apps you use to find your hookups has a BFF side, where you can connect with people looking for strong female relationships.

- Volunteering—Find a cause you love & volunteer. We've made so many quality life-long friends through volunteerism.

Behind every successful woman is a tribe of other successful women who have her back, women who know how to do life in heels backward.

So Super Squad-Up, Girl!

***

Journal Prompt #19

Make a list of all the amazing women in your life. Write their names & something you can do to support them. (This can be as simple as sharing their next project on social media or texting them happy birthday each year).

If you look at that list & it seems a little light to you—that's okay! You've now identified that you need more badass women in your life, & the great thing is they are out there looking for you. Starting a community project, volunteering, hobby groups, or fitness activities can be a great way to meet like-minded witches.

AFFIRMATION

I attract amazing people into my life who make my world bigger.

(Say this phrase in a mirror until it makes you smile)

Pin-Ups On Tour Performers volunteering during the Holidays at the Las Vegas VA Medical Center in 2016. Pictured: Kitty Kat DeMille, Julia Reed Nichols, Natalie Rose White, Veteran @ center, Buddy Watson, Harley Harpurr, Jessi-Belle & Dixie Mae Rebel

19 - IT'S OKAY TO MAKE OTHERS JEALOUS; YOU'RE ACTUALLY GIVING THEM A GIFT!

> Don't worry about the people who aren't happy for you.
> They probably aren't happy for themselves either.
>
> —*Unknown*

This might sound a little strange, but jealousy is actually a gift. It's your gift to inspire people to be more.

What if you heard that your friend went to Fiji? You might be jealous to hear that they had that experience, but over time, that trip might inspire you to be more adventurous & book a ticket to Fiji. But you would have never booked that ticket unless there was a moment where you were jealous of your friend.

When someone judges you in any way, it isn't actually about you. It's about them & their own insecurities, limitations, & needs. Jealousy is just a lack of self-confidence, a case of the Drabbies.

Also remember that jealousy is only a frame on the film reel of life & everyone is on their own Magical path. Yesterday's jealousy is today's motivation & tomorrow's success.

We'll all get there when we're meant to. Until then, feel for these people, but then go back to sparkling, shining, & being exactly who you were meant to be.

***

Journal Prompt #20

Are there people in your life you are jealous of? What parts of them make you jealous? How can you foster those traits in yourself? Can you learn to celebrate those traits in others as inspiration?

AFFIRMATION

I notice the good traits in others that I have in myself.

(Say this in the mirror until the phrase makes you smile)

GREEN EYED MONSTER by Julia Reed Nichols

20 - ROCK & ROLL CAN SAVE YOUR SOUL

> Music is a safe kind of high.
>
> —*Jimi Hendrix*

Sometimes music is the only medicine the heart & soul need.

Music is what feelings sound like. It is a piece of art that goes in the ears & straight to the heart. It has the power to make us smile, to bring us to tears, & help us realize the answers. It can carry us back in time & inspire us to dance in the moment. For all our happiest moments as a human being, there is music. Weddings, graduations, & Burlesque shows, music is always there.

Music can be the cure for the noise your mind drowns in. If you're having a bad day, you can reset the story by playing some peppy music. And like Magic, your mind is off your problem.

Music has the ability to change how you think, literally. A recent scientific research study found that music is so influential on the brain that the type you listen to actually has the ability to alter the way you process information. These science geeks discovered that the more convergent the music you listen to, the more harmonious your thinking will be. Conversely, the more dissonant the music, the more discordant & fragmented your mind becomes.

Which means that music is one of the most powerful ways to quickly change your state of being. It is the most Magical mood changer ever. Music has profound effects on emotions, inducing states of relaxation, which are particularly useful as an antidote to depression, anxiety, & fatigue.

Listening is the most basic of ways, but if you want to alter your state even quicker, you actively interact with music in such ways as:

- **SINGING**

Singing is one of the simplest & yet most powerful forms of music-making. Every human being is born with the capacity to sing in a way that aligns their inner & outer messages, freeing the soul. Musical notes create vibrations that combine in bigger forms to create melodies. When singing is combined with positive uplifting lyrics, it can send messages to your brain, & the rest of your body can literally change your physical & molecular composition for the better.

- **DANCING**

Dance is one of the most primal of self-expressions, so don't judge how it bursts forth. Just move! Don't focus on anyone else, for it's only you & your dance partner: the music. Turn up the volume, close your eyes, & let the music take over your soul. Let it emerge however it needs to. Toe tapping, finger snapping, hips wiggling, there's really no right or wrong way.

- **DRUMMING**

The drum is a deep & sacred element of self-expression in many cultures. In scientific studies, it's been discovered that the process of drumming engages both the linear, rational left side of the brain & the creative, intuitive right side of the brain. Although the two brain hemispheres often emanate different wave frequencies, drumming, like deep meditation, brings them into synchronization, creating feelings of euphoria & flowing creativity.

Also, make sure to explore the diverse Universes of music. People who listen to several different genres of music tend to be more honest, loyal, intelligent, & great decision makers.

As Bob Marley said, "the good thing about music, once it hits you, you feel no pain."

***

Journal Prompt #21

Pick your favorite "feel like a badass song." (Julia's is Gangsters Paradise by Coolio for the record) Play it & enjoy it. Pay it again. This time write about what that song means to you, why you love it, what emotions it invokes, what sentimental attachments are associated with it, where do you feel it in your body, & how it makes you want to move.

AFFIRMATION

Music is my medicine & I take it daily.

(Say this phrase in the mirror until you smile)

The Green Light District performing at a private party at MJ BizCon, the world's largest cannabis trade show, in 2019. Pictured: Julia Reed Nichols, Erin Baltsar & Jay Yaskin

21 - IF YOU CAN APPRECIATE YOUR ASSETS, YOU'LL ALWAYS SHOW A PROFIT!

> Love & appreciation are identical vibrations. Appreciation is the vibration of alignment with who-you-are. Appreciation is the absence of everything that feels bad & the presence of everything that feels good.
>
> —*Abraham-Hicks*

The more appreciative you are, the more beauty that you can see.

Appreciation is the gateway into a Magical world of wonder. It helps you see what there is, instead of what there isn't. And when it becomes the base foundation in our lives, Magic starts to appear everywhere.

Appreciation is also a powerful catalyst for happiness. But to make it work, you need to start RIGHT NOW. For if you aren't appreciative for what you already have, what makes you think you'd be better off with more?

Appreciation turns what we have into enough, which allows more to come in.

***

Journal Prompt #22

Making a list of what you are appreciative for is a great first step, but to come full circle, you need to start noticing these moments in your everyday life. Think of a regular day, write your tasks start to finish—from waking up, to brushing your teeth, to driving to work, & so on. Next to each activity, find something to be appreciative for & notice in the moment.

An example of this would be, "When I drink my coffee, I am appreciative of the smell that helps wake me up." (Or maybe the mug you drink it out of is amazing!) Making this list will help connect those neuro-pathways in your head, making appreciation a habit.

AFFIRMATION

I have so much to be appreciative for.

(Say this phrase in the mirror until it makes you smile)

The first Green Light District @ The Crest Theater in Los Angeles benefiting Pin-Ups for Vets - Pictured: Kat Thomas, Siren Noire, Julia Reed Nichols, Ricky Reba, Gina Elise, Jessi Belle, Jessabelle Thunder, Tonya Kay, DJ Skylar Gilmore, Dixie Mae Rebel & Buddy Watson

22 - DREAMS ARE FOREVER & IMAGINATION HAS NO AGE

I think it's your mental attitude. So many of us start dreading age in high school, & that's a waste of a lovely life. "Oh. . . I'm 30, Oh, I'm 40, Oh, 50."

Make the most of it.

—Betty White

Giving up is the birth of regret & the death of Magic.

So many of us focus on everything needing to happen right away, & when it doesn't, we get disappointed. We get bitter. We stop trusting in the Magic of The Universe.

We fear failure, citing it most often for our reason for never trying. But failure is the only way we learn, the only way we grow. Don't give up because of one bad chapter in your life, your story doesn't end here. Or here. Or here. It keeps going, & going, & going.

And because it keeps going, & going, & going, nothing is ever really a big deal.

Every time we fall down as kids, it's a learning lesson on how to get back up. With failure comes persistence, something that can only be learned through contrast experiences.

It's okay to not be okay; just don't give up. Everything is hard before it is easy.

Your dream doesn't have an expiration date so take a deep breath & try again.

If the plan doesn't work, change the plan, but never the goal. Thomas Edison noted when discussing his invention of the light bulb, "I have not failed. I've just found 10,000 ways that won't work." Each time Edison discovered a way not to create a lightbulb, it focused him more on discovering a way it would work.

You are always going to dream about more, that's the nature of an expanding Universe. But you don't want every single thing on your wish list to arrive all on the same day. Where is the mystery & Magic in that?

Instead, think about the world of the world. Hold the vision & trust the process, because The Universe has your back.

Don't give up on your dreams & they won't give up on you.

***

Journal Prompt #23

How does fear of failure show up in your life? Noticing is the first step to changing your approach, so give yourself an honest assessment. Was there a big move you didn't make? Businesses you didn't open? People you didn't say you loved? Notice where you made the risk-averse choice, & maybe you will make a different one next time.

AFFIRMATION

I don't quit, I evolve.

(Say this phrase in a mirror until it makes you smile)

Behind the Scenes from WTT Burly's Legend Documentary in Partnership with The Burlesque Hall of Fame. Pictured: Kitty Kat DeMille, Burlesque LEGEND Dee Milo, & Julia Reed Nichols

ROMANCE

23 - RELATIONSHIPS ARE THE ULTIMATE LESSON IN WHO WE ARE

The greatest gift you can ever give another person is your own happiness.

—Abraham-Hicks

Relationships are lessons in who we are.

Relationships are mirrors where we see the good, the bad, & ugly so we can grow & evolve as people. That being said, you really want to be in relationships where you're consistently seeing 85 percent Good, 10 percent Bad, & 5 percent Ugly.

Relationships don't always have to be easy, but there should be an ease to them. Which means finding a Sweetie who's easy to love. We should all be with someone who ruins your lipstick, not your mascara.

A healthy relationship is where two independent people just make a deal that they will help make the other person the best version of themselves. But for that to work, you need to know who you are, know who you don't want to be, & know who you are going to be.

Make yourself a priority in your relationship. You're the only one who knows your standards, & once you know them, you must effectively communicate them. Don't make exceptions on your boundaries.

If you feel uncomfortable with your Sweetheart's words or deeds, you must talk to them. You cannot change situations by only loving them harder. You must tell them that their actions do not live up to your standards. The best relationships are constantly exchanging information so each party can course correct. The result is you both become better versions of yourselves.

As a general rule of thumb, our mantra is: Only date people you'd be happy seeing your Bestie dating! If the person you're seeing is in any way someone you would try & talk your girlfriend into breaking up with, then you need to move on to greener pastures.

REPEAT AFTER US: Fuck This! I Deserve Better!

We know you deserve the best The Universe has to offer, but the only way The Universe can Magically bestow it on you is for you to believe you deserve it.

As the saying goes, "God can't give you a diamond if you are holding onto a clump of coal."

***

Journal Prompt #24

What does being loved feel like to you? In your dream world—what do you want in your Sweetheart? How is romantic love currently reflected in your life? Where is there room to ask for more? (Or celebrate the person who is already giving it to you!)

AFFIRMATION

Love feels good.

(Say this phrase in a mirror until you are smiling)

FUCK IT by Amber Schindler

24 - CONFIDENCE IS GRAVITATIONAL

> She had the one essential star quality:
> she could be magnificent at doing nothing.
>
> —*German actress Lili Darvas on Marlene Dietrich*

Thinking you're less than someone doesn't work when you're on stage. . . or in life. Beauty pulls things toward you in a way that lack & limitation could never do. But you need to believe that for it to work.

You need to constantly think you're more & more will come your way. Many women lose their power when they start chasing after something. When they feel that they're always two steps behind & can never catch up.

So STOP chasing that proverbial carrot. You'd be surprised how much strength you'll get from just standing still.

One of the moves that can be the hardest to learn as a Burlesque Performer is just standing still on stage. When most of us first start out as performers, we come up with tons of busy work—extra dance moves, tons of costume pieces to remove, etc., to fill the time. But once mastered, the art of standing still, can be one of the boldest moves in your performer wheelhouse.

Think of yourself as a beautiful piece of art that should be hanging in a museum. If you're not thinking yourself to be that rare, you're missing the point: people should pay to stand in your presence. This payment can come in whatever form you want, we're partial to movie contracts & diamonds, but compliments work just as well.

And this doesn't mean you shouldn't be a thoroughly modern woman & be aggressive in regards to what you want. We love empowered people who speak up & ask for what they want. But don't tie the result to your self-worth. We know too many women out there who make moves normally deemed masculine such as asking Sweetheart out or initiating telecommunications (text, phone call, any & all social platforms), but then question their actions when they don't get the response they were hoping for.

Either way, the best course of action is to know what you want & what you can control. If you're a Girly Girl who chooses to let the Sweetie she's been flirting with ask her out, that's okay. But if you're the more Assertive Type, who schedules her date out, that is totally cool too. Just know who you are & embrace it thoroughly.

You do you, Boo, in the most authentic way possible.

***

Journal Prompt #25

The first step to tapping into who you are is to look within. If you don't have a daily meditation practice, we highly recommend starting one. For now, take a few minutes to tune in & listen to yourself. The first step in getting what you want is getting clear! Start by slowing down & becoming present in the moment. Find a comfortable position, back supported. If you have access to music & essential oils, we highly recommend involving them into your practice. Tune into the sounds around you, the feeling of the clothing on your body (or the air on your skin if you are naked!), & feeling of the breath in your body. Give yourself ten cycles of square breathing—Count of four, IN; Count of four, HOLD; Count of four, OUT; Count of four, HOLD. Return to normal breathing. Mentally ask yourself "What do I want?" & allow yourself to journal or speak aloud what you want The Universe to bring forth.

AFFIRMATION

Going within feels good.

(Say this in the mirror until the phrase makes you smile)

SHOWGIRL MAGIC by Kitty Kat DeMille

25 - WORK THE TEASE

The Universe operates through dynamic exchange. . . Giving & receiving are different aspects of the flow of energy in The Universe. And in our willingness to give that which we seek, we keep the abundance of The Universe circulating in our lives.

—*Deepak Chopra*

Make it your goal to brighten everyone's day; it will come back tenfold!

Flirt with Life! Members of the Glitterati are never self-absorbed. Their gaze is directed outward, not inward. Drabsters are always protecting the tiny realm of their own lives, constantly strategizing to protect their safety.

<u>True members of the Glitterati never strategize.</u>

Instead, every interaction, whether personal, social, or career related, is seen as a potential opportunity to seduce with FUN.

So have a warrior witch's outlook when it comes to all who surround you. Helping them to smile is the best spell you can ever cast.

So hurry, there isn't a moment to waste. Make love to the world, You Magical Witch!!

***

Journal Prompt #26

How do you feel about the idea of flirting in the world? Where can you be more playful in life? Where can you love more?

AFFIRMATION

It feels good to give & receive love.

(Say this in the mirror until the phrase makes you smile)

Pin-Ups On Tour's TIki For The Troops @ Don The Beachcombers in Huntington Beach. Pictured: Kitty Kat DeMille, Siren Noire, Dixie Mae Rebel & Vixen DeVille

26 - EMBRACE MYSTERY

If a thing is worth doing, it is worth doing slowly. . . very slowly.

—*Gypsy Rose Lee*

There is true power in being subtle.

Mystery is an art form that most modern women have forgotten. There is such strength in making people wonder what you're thinking.

Now we absolutely love it when women speak their mind, & we absolutely embrace this a hundred times over! But speaking to fill the silence because you are uncomfortable is another story. . .

As the saying goes: you were given two ears & one mouth; use them accordingly.

In silence, you become interesting, mysterious, & Magical. You become something to be figured out, an enigma to be solved.

***

Journal Prompt #27

Are there places in your life where you might benefit with more silence? Or at least taking a bit more time to respond? In Business? In relationships?

AFFIRMATION

I take time to enjoy things.

(Say this in the mirror until the phrase makes you smile)

Gypsy Rose Lee "cut out" in action @ The Drawing Room in Las Vegas, NV for Workin' The Tease: Private Sessions Burlesque

27 - SEX MAGIC IS REAL

An orgasm a day keeps the doctor away.

—*Mae West*

Two & you'll never feel blue! ;-)

—*Pinup Julia*

Turns out your orgasms are Magic!

Sex Magic is an ancient manifestation practice that amplifies your intentions with the energetic power of an orgasm. It helps you bring your dreams into waking life through orgasmic vibrations that intensify clarity & focus. Sounds like fun, right?

Sex is like a jungle gym for adults. Once you're invited to the playground, why would you ever want to go back to the baby swings? Orgasms make life Magical so try & get them any way you can! Get to know your body, what makes it happy & what doesn't. You first need to know what Turns You On. Which means playing with yourself. Which means masturbating. Now there might be some of you reading this book that have issues with masturbation. That you feel it's wrong in some way, that it's a sin against your religion, against your Sweetie, or maybe you're slightly paranoid that it will turn you blind like some weird relative told you it would (BTW: It won't, we typed this book perfectly fine!).

And if you harbor the belief that there is something wrong with you making yourself feel good, we wholeheartedly suggest you find the best way to get over that ASAP; whether it be therapy, doing some Ayahuasca in the jungle, or just spending hours having a Menage a Moi.

This might sound a bit redundant, but playing with yourself is about play.

It's about exploring your body so you have the ability to share it. It also allows you to train yourself so you know how to climax. Nobody outside of you will ever give you an orgasm. Others can help aid you, but you're in charge of your own physical happiness. Think of them as friends giving you a ride home from a party. Sure, they've got the car, but you're not going to get anywhere if you don't know your own address.

That being said, we know how important our Magical Os are, so we do have some great tips for traversing the climax of that mountain, either solo or with a partner.

- **DO YOU HAVE THE TIME?**

For the majority of women, the most sensitive part of the clitoris is the upper left-hand quadrant from their body's perspective. Or from your Sweetie's perspective about one o'clock. Get very familiar with this area as it will be the rainbow you follow to your pot of gold!

- **THE EDGE OF THE WORLD**

The longer you build up arousal, the bigger the explosion. Known as the technique of Edging, when cooking your orgasm, get yourself close to a boil & then knock yourself back to a simmer. Repeat this a few times before you climax & you experience what the French called a Petit Mort, the little death that happens when your orgasm has blown your mind to bits.

- **FRICTION IS YOUR FRIEND**

70 percent of American women don't experience orgasms from intercourse. So to make the odds ever in your favor, you need to find a friction position. Get on top, letting the top of your clitoris rub directly on Sweetheart's pubic bone. Or lay on your back with a pillow underneath your seat. Rule of thumb, the woman applies the movement, while the other dance partner supplies the pressure. And there's always a girl's best friend, her vibrator!

- **BREATH**

Remember what Miss Ophelia Flame stated about lack of breathing? Well, turns out it's pretty important during sex too! Breathing allows oxygen to circulate around the body, which is necessary when dealing in the world of sexy time. Use your breath to channel your sexual energy. Respiratory Tango with your Sweetheart by breathing in tandem, the results are slowing the rush to orgasm, which creates a bigger buildup that leads to a better bang for your buck!

- **BE A RISK TAKER**

Research shows that thrill-seeking adventures with a Sweetie from skydiving to going to the amusement park to just going to see a scary movie stimulate dopamine in the brain, which gets you in the mood for some adventures in the bedroom!

- **HIT THE GYM FOR YOUR VAGINA**

Strengthen your pelvic floor by practicing your Kegels. The pelvic floor muscles are the foundation for the core of the body so make sure you've got it as strong as possible. The easiest way to locate the muscles in your pelvic floor is by stopping yourself from peeing midstream. Then tone them by clenching when you're outside the loo. Like that proverbial apple, make sure to do your Kegel every day. And don't forget to breathe during rehearsals; otherwise, you won't be ready for the Olympics.

- **GEMSTONES FOR YOUR VAJAYJAY**

Jade Eggs are also a fantastic opportunity for exploration! Asian women have used these stone eggs for centuries to tighten vaginal muscles. As time went on, the secret of this practice was housed inside the Chinese Royal Palace & was taught only to the queen & concubines. Many who mastered the Jade Egg technique appeared to have drunk from the fountain of youth with vaginas in old age as "tight & strong as unmarried maids." As a healing stone, Jade works with the heart chakra & promotes self-realization & self-reliance. Like the aforementioned Kegels, Jade Eggs strengthens the floor of your sexual organs allowing for better control of the vagina, bladder, & rectum, along with the ability to do vaginal Kung-Fu grip for Fan-Fucking-Tastic Sex!

- **BE COMFORTABLE WITH THE MESS**

Sex isn't pretty. Get comfortable with your O-Face in all its scrunched-up Cabbage Patch Kids glory. Remember that Porn, like Hollywood movies, is not real. No one has "pretty" orgasms. If you want to see what real sex looks like, check out Beautiful Agony, a website that began as a multimedia experiment to test a hypothesis that eroticism in human imagery rests not in nakedness, but our engagement with the face. Since 2003, they have been uploading videos of people having orgasms from the neck up, no nakedness, just facial ecstasy. So embrace the sweaty hair, the loud moans, the blotchy red skin, & a face full of surprised expressions; they show you're in it to win it.

***

Journal Prompt #28

Masturbate in a new way—yup, it is time to experiment! Find a new toy, place, or object of inspiration—maybe even play with your Sweetheart & enjoy the sensation of experiencing something new. What did it feel like? What else do you want to experiment with? Once you open the door for sexual exploration, we encourage you to walk through it & explore!

AFFIRMATION

Sex is FUN; I'm great at it.

(Say this in the mirror until the phrase makes you smile)

Julia & Kat at Las Vegas PRIDE Parade

28 - PROTECT YOUR BOUNDARIES

You are not required to set yourself on fire to keep others warm.

—Unknown

You are in charge of your life, no one else. Which means you need to learn to communicate your standards & boundaries.

Your Yes's & No's are the commodities of communication, so make sure you're spending both tools equally well.

Many people have issues saying "No" to someone else mainly because they want to please the person in front of them. But this only hinders all parties involved.

You have the right to say No.

No is a very powerful word as it is both a communication tool & a barrier for your protection. It establishes agency by creating your line in the sand. It declares, this is Who-I-Am & this is What-I-Value.

HOW TO SAY NO:

- Assess The Situation.
- Be Quick.
- Be Honest.
- Suggest an Alternative.
- Ask for a Raincheck.

Relationships only work when we are honest with ourselves & others. Which means we must communicate our standards as effectively as possible.

Over the years, we have discovered some enchanting words that can help communicate appreciation or when you might need to course correct your relationship a bit.

MAGIC WORDS OF APPRECIATION:

- Thank You.
- I Love It When. . .

- It's Sexy When. . .

- It Turns Me On When. . .

- You Are So Respectful Of Me When You. . .

MAGIC WORDS TO COURSE CORRECT

- It Makes Me Feel Less Loved When. . .

- Try & Put Yourself In My Shoes. . .

- I'm Gonna Lay Out My Argument & You Tell Me Where I'm Wrong. . .

- I See Where You Are Coming From. . .

- Here's My Issue With That. . .

- I Feel Really Bad When. . .

- I Feel Really Left Out When. . .

How they respond will show you the direction your relationship is going. And Glitterati Pro-Communicator tip, own your feelings & avoid assuming how the other person may have felt in a conversation.

THE WITCHY WAY TO WORD CONSTRUCTIVE FEEDBACK:

When You Did *<u>Identifiable Action/Behavior Here</u>*, It Made Me Feel *<u>Your Emotion Here</u>*.

This way you are owning your experience & giving the other person room to speak their true intentions. (Because rarely it is the story we have made up in our head).

Please note, your perfect Sweetie isn't one who does everything right, but one who is willing to work on themselves & evolve for the good of the relationship.

***

Journal Prompt #29

Think about a difficult conversation you need to have. Now write out that conversation using the tools above as a guide. Sometimes having a script gives us permission to approach the task.

AFFIRMATION

I speak clearly.

(Say this phrase in the mirror until it makes you smile)

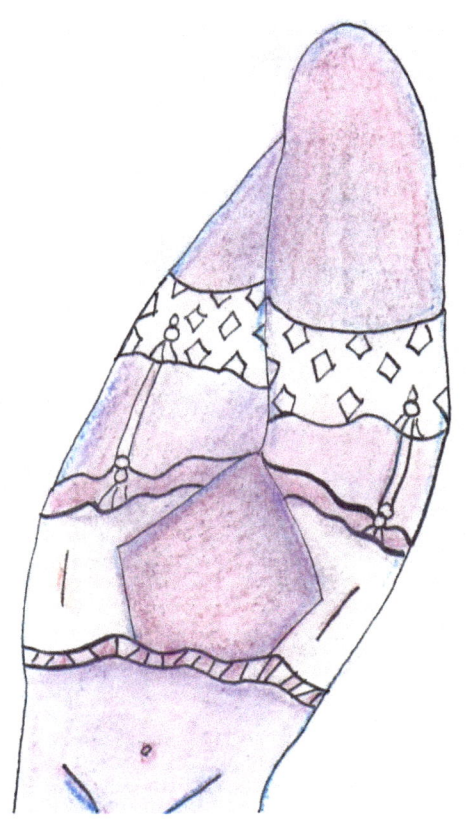

MY JOB IS JUST TO BE PRETTY, AND ISN'T THAT AWESOME by Kitty Kat DeMille

29 - IT TAKES TWO TO TANGO

> Live life as if everything is rigged in your favor.
>
> —*Rumi*

Dating is the art of finding two people who want to dance together. And like dancing, both parties must be properly paired for as they say: it takes two to tango.

Every person has specific standards in a variety of categories such as family, health, work, money, loyalty, religion/spirituality, & physical attraction/sexuality. These standards define you as a human being. They are what makes you "you."

Which means to dance, you need to find someone who matches you in most categories. It doesn't need to be 100 percent, but overall, a letter grade that you would have been proud to bring home to your parents in high school. Think A+ to B+ range.

Compatibility is defined as the ability to exist together in harmony. Which means you must find a Sweetheart who shares whatever values you hold. There's no excuse for low standards in a relationship. No matter how much you love someone, you should never settle for less than you deserve.

Your relationship is a mirror of who you are, so when you look at your reflection you should see beauty, inside & out.

The ideal Sweetie is one who brings out the best in you. Who boosts your self-esteem & pushes you forward to become your best self. You deserve to feel loved, & safe, & happy when you're in a relationship.

***

Journal Prompt #30

What are your relationship Standards? Put them on paper & honor them. You'll thank us later, we promise!

AFFIRMATION

I have high standards.

(Say this phrase in the mirror until it makes you smile)

Tango by Amber Schindler

THE ONLY RULE

30 - CHANGE IS THE ONLY CONSTANT

I'm not the type to sit on the porch & watch life go by.

—*Sally Rand*

Don't compare your surface beauty of the past to the surface beauty of today. Because at the end of the day, neither of them was real. In case you haven't heard, Beauty is an Inside Job.

Live in the moment because this is the only moment you'll get with it. Don't let it pass you by.

Unhappiness comes from living in the past or the future, of not fully being in the present. Whether it be about looking at a picture of what we looked like ten years ago or hoping we'll someday fit into that dress that is two sizes smaller than we are right now. Helen Mirren is the Sexiest Most Magical thing out there in her seventies because she's living in the skin she's in right now.

As we've mentioned before, Workin' The Tease absolutely loves the Friday night Titans of Tease performances at the BHoF weekend aka Legends Night. There is nothing more amazing than seeing a ninety-year-old woman strip in front of a crowd of more than 500 people to a standing ovation.

When we interviewed Burlesque legend Madame E, age sixty-two, in our "Taking It Off In Your Golden Years" episode, she said how wonderful it felt. "The first time I did it as an Oldster, as a Legend, it just brought back so many wonderful memories. And when the audience started cheering, I just cried; it just felt so good."

Which doesn't mean these women don't have their own issues with the aging process. The eighty-one-year-old Penny Starr Sr. (Grandmother to Penny Starr Jr) commented on how, "There's a lot of moves I can't do anymore because I'm afraid if I get down, I can't get back up."

But these women are still Magic on stage, because this is who they are.

Empowerment is found through showing off who you truly are. You are who you are in this moment. So, be naked in everything you do & are.
You are beautiful because you are you.

***

Journal Prompt #31

Where do you go from here? Do you give yourself permission to start that business? Do you open yourself up to love? Do you take that Burlesque class? Give yourself permission to take the lessons of this book into every part of your life & get naked more!

AFFIRMATION

Beauty is an inside job.

(Say this in the mirror until the phrase makes you smile)

BEAUTY IS AN INSIDE JOB by Amber Schindler

NAMASTE BITCHES!

Follow Our Adventures

PODCAST
Better Than Sex

INSTAGRAM
@WTTBurly

YOUTUBE
www.youtube.com/wttburly

WEBSITE
www.WTTBurlesque.com

OUR OTHER BRANDS

The Green Light District

The Event People Creative Co-Op

The Drawing Room Foundation

The Zelda Fitzgeralds

Pin-Ups on Tour

This Way Adventures

Edible Skinny

www.ingramcontent.com/pod-product-compliance
Lightning Source LLC
Chambersburg PA
CBHW061756290426
44109CB00030B/2872